D0574848

MILITARY HELICOPTERS
Flying into Battle

Lynn Peppas

⚜ Crabtree Publishing Company

www.crabtreebooks.com

Created by Bobbie Kalman

Author
Lynn Peppas

Editor
Adrianna Morganelli

Proofreader
Kathy Middleton

Photo research
Samara Parent

Design
Samara Parent

**Production coordinator
and prepress technician**
Samara Parent

Print coordinator
Katherine Berti

Photographs

Shutterstock.com: front cover; © TebNad (title page); © 1971yes (page 4);
© Keith Tarrier (page 5); © Sharon Hitman (pages 6-7); © Simon Krzic (page 8);
© Shamleen (page 9); © steve estvanik (page 10); © JustASC (page 11 both);
© Jordan Tan (page 13); © Dan Simonsen (page 14 bottom);
© Mauro (page 15); © Yen Hung Lin (page 17 both); © Stephen Coburn
(page 20 bottom); © Arie v.d. Wolde (pages 20-21); © Dariusz Majgier
(page 23 both); © Liv Falvey (pages 26-27); © jathys (page 28);
© Ian Edward Schofield (page 29 bottom); page 29 top; © Johnny Dao
(page 29)

Thinkstock.com: Contents page

Wikimedia Commons: © Alan Radecki (back cover); © Serendipity (page 14 top);
© Cezary Piwowarski (page 25); U.S. Army: pages 12, 16, 18-19, 22, 24, 30

Front cover: A close up view of the front of an Apache helicopter

Back cover: A U.S. Air Force MH-60 Blackhawk

Title page: Three Ah-64d Apache helicopters fly through the sky at sunset

Library and Archives Canada Cataloguing in Publication

Peppas, Lynn
    Military helicopters : flying into battle / Lynn Peppas.

(Vehicles on the move)
Includes index.
Issued also in electronic formats.
ISBN 978-0-7787-2749-1 (bound).--ISBN 978-0-7787-2754-5 (pbk.)

    1. Military helicopters--Juvenile literature.
I. Title. II. Series: Vehicles on the move

UG1230.P46 2011   j623.74'6047   C2011-906691-2

Library of Congress Cataloging-in-Publication Data

Peppas, Lynn.
    Military helicopters : flying into battle / Lynn Peppas.
        p. cm. -- (Vehicles on the move)
    Includes index.
    Audience: Ages 5-8.
    ISBN 978-0-7787-2749-1 (library binding : alk. paper) -- ISBN 978-0-7787-
2754-5 (pbk. : alk. paper) -- ISBN 978-1-4271-9927-0 (.pdf) -- ISBN 978-1-
4271-9932-4 (electronic html)
    1. Military helicopters--Juvenile literature. I. Title. II. Series.

    UG1230.P37 2012
    358.4'183--dc23
                                        2011039602

Crabtree Publishing Company

Printed in the U.S.A./112011/JA20111018

www.crabtreebooks.com   1-800-387-7650

**Published in Canada
Crabtree Publishing**
616 Welland Ave.
St. Catharines, Ontario
L2M 5V6

**Published in the United States
Crabtree Publishing**
PMB 59051
350 Fifth Avenue, 59th Floor
New York, New York 10118

**Published in the United Kingdom
Crabtree Publishing**
Maritime House
Basin Road North, Hove
BN41 1WR

**Published in Australia
Crabtree Publishing**
3 Charles Street
Coburg North
VIC 3058

Contents

Military Helicopters

Military helicopters are vehicles that fly. Vehicles are machines that move people and things. Military vehicles do important jobs for a country's **armed forces**. A helicopter is also called an aircraft.

Sometimes helicopters are called "choppers," because of the chopping sound they make when the rotor blades turn.

Military helicopters are used to keep watch over certain areas. They move soldiers and weapons from one place to another. Some attack **enemy** targets on the ground or at sea. They also look for and rescue people in trouble. Military helicopters have special **armor** to protect them during attacks. They come in many different shapes and sizes.

Parts of a Military Helicopter

Helicopters can fly almost anywhere. They get up in the air with overhead rotor blades that **rotate**, or spin around, at fast speeds. They can take off and land almost anywhere. They do not need a long runway to get off the ground like most airplanes or jets do.

rotor blades

tail rotor

main rotor

engine

tail boom

921

Helicopters can move in more ways than a jet or any other vehicle. They fly up or down, backward, forward, and sideways. Airplanes cannot fly sideways or backward like a helicopter can. Helicopters can also **hover**, or stay in one place in the air.

drive shaft

cockpit

921

Military Helicopter Pilots

People who fly helicopters are called pilots. Flying a helicopter is one of the hardest and most dangerous jobs. Pilots must use their hands and feet at the same time to fly a helicopter.

Pilots sit in an area at the front of the helicopter called the cockpit.

helmet with sun visor

life vest

Pilots wear special gear to keep them safe when flying a helicopter. They wear flight suits and sometimes life vests, as well as special flight boots and gloves. They also wear helmets through which they can talk, hear, and get **information**.

flight suit

flight boots

9

Attack Helicopters

Attack helicopters do just what their name says. They attack enemy forces on the ground, at sea, or in the air. Military attack helicopters carry weapons such as guns, rockets, and missiles. Rockets and missiles are weapons that travel through the air. They explode when they hit something.

The Super Cobra is a military attack helicopter. It has a **crew** of one pilot and one gunner. A gunner fires the weapons. It can fly up to speeds of 218 mph (350 km/h).

*Below the cockpit, the Super Cobra has special **sensors** that help the gunner aim and fire weapons.*

Apache Attack Helicopter

The Apache helicopter is made for ground attacks. It was originally designed for attacking tanks. It has a crew of one pilot and one gunner. It has a big gun called a cannon underneath that points wherever the gunner is looking. It is controlled by the gunner through his or her helmet.

An Apache attack helicopter can fly over 190 mph (305 km/h).

The Apache carries rockets and missiles. It can fly and attack at night. It has special armor to protect it during **combat**. It has short wings with heavy weapons, such as missile or rocket **launchers**, attached.

Mangusta Attack Helicopter

The Mangusta helicopter is ready to fight anytime. It flies and fights at night or in bad weather. It fights other aircraft in the air. It also fights enemy forces on the ground.

The Mangusta can fly at speeds of up to 173 mph (278 km/h).

It takes two people to operate the Mangusta. The pilot sits above and behind the gunner. The gunner operates a cannon, located under the nose of the helicopter, and missiles. The Mangusta's rotor blades are almost 40 feet (12 m) long.

pilot

gunner

cannon

Scout Helicopter

Not all military helicopters are used to attack. Some, like the Kiowa, are used to scout, or observe, an area to get information. They can fly up to speeds of 147 mph (237 km/h).

Although mainly used for scouting, the Kiowa Warrior can also shoot at targets. It carries a machine gun, rockets, and missiles.

The Kiowa has something called mast-mounted sight (MMS). This giant ball on top of the main rotor can see everything around— even at night or in bad weather. The helicopter is able to hide behind cover during ground combat and still see enemy targets. It then shares the information with soldiers on the ground.

MMS

Transport Helicopters

Some military helicopters are used to transport, or move, heavy weapons and armed forces. The Super Stallion is one of the biggest heavy-lift transport helicopters in the U.S. military. A stallion is a powerful, male horse. Long ago, horses were used to move people and things. Today, the Super Stallion helicopter moves both people and extremely heavy military equipment.

Super Stallions have seven rotor blades that help them lift heavy loads. The aircraft is often called the Hurricane Maker because they create a lot of wind.

The Super Stallion can travel at speeds up to 196 mph (315 km/h). Transport helicopters carry loads inside the aircraft, or outside hanging in a large sling. The Super Stallion can carry up to 30,000 pounds (13,600 kg) on the inside or 36,000 pounds (16,300 kg) on the outside.

The Chinook is another heavy-lift transport helicopter. Sometimes it is called a cargo helicopter. Cargo is another word for a load of goods carried by a vehicle. The CH-47 Chinook has two main rotors: one on the front and another on the back. Each rotor has three rotor blades.

The Chinook has a wide loading ramp at the back of the helicopter and three hooks on the outside to carry cargo.

The Chinook can land on water or ground. It can carry up to 28,000 pounds (12,700 kg) of cargo. It has three machine guns and is able to carry weapons such as missiles to protect it from an attack.

Each Chinook costs about 35 million dollars.

Anti-Submarine Helicopter

The Super Seasprite is a helicopter that is used at sea. It can take off and land from an aircraft carrier or warship. An aircraft carrier is a ship that stores and launches aircraft such as the Seasprite.

The Super Seasprite was used in Operation Desert Storm in the Persian Gulf in 1991. They have since been replaced in the U.S. Navy by the Seahawk.

The Super Seasprite has special machines that help it find things underwater that people cannot see. It can find things such as enemy submarines or **underwater mines**. It can fire missiles or torpedoes. It can travel at speeds up to 159 mph (256 km/h).

(right) Super Seasprite cockpit

(below) SH-2G Super Seasprite

Multi-Role Helicopters

Some military helicopters do more than one job. They are called multi-role military helicopters. The Mi-24 Hind is an attack helicopter that is bigger than most attack helicopters. It carries cargo or armed forces, too.

The Mi-24 Hind can hold up to eight soldiers.

The Hind has a cannon, machine guns, rockets, and missiles. It has short wings on the sides that carry some of the weapons. It cannot hover like other attack helicopters, but it is faster than most military helicopters.

The Mi-24 Hind can travel at speeds up to 208 mph (335 km/h).

Eurocopter Tiger

The Eurocopter Tiger is a multi-role military helicopter. It is used to scout areas. Some have a mast-mounted site that can see things that people cannot. It is also used as an attack helicopter. It has a built-in cannon in the helicopter's nose. It also has short, stubby wings that carry rocket and missile launchers.

It takes two people to fly the Eurocopter Tiger. The pilot sits in the front and the gunner sits behind. It can fly up to speeds of almost 180 mph (290 km/h). They cost about 40 million dollars.

Special Operations Tiltrotors

A special operations force is a special team or group of people in the military. They are trained to do jobs that are especially dangerous or hard to do. Special operations forces often use a tiltrotor aircraft called the Osprey. A tiltrotor aircraft has wings, but can move up and down, as well as hover, like a helicopter.

The Osprey can travel at speeds up to 315 mph (509 km/h).

The Osprey is a big aircraft. It has two wings, like a jet, with rotors on the end of each wing. These rotors can tilt, or move in different directions. This allows the aircraft to hover like a helicopter, as well as take off or land in a small area. The Osprey can, however, fly faster and travel farther than a regular helicopter.

*An Osprey's wings can be turned in and the rotors can be folded up to save space when parked on an **aircraft carrier**.*

Black Hawk

The Black Hawk is used for many jobs. It is sometimes called the **workhorse** of the U.S. Army. A special operations rescue model is called the Pave Hawk. There are Rescue Hawks, Seahawks, and Knighthawks, too. All use the same Black Hawk frame but have special weapons or scouting machines added to them for special jobs.

A Seahawk performs during training exercises.

Black Hawks can carry heavy loads. They are **armed** with machine guns. It takes two pilots to fly the aircraft, and it can hold two gunners. Black Hawks can carry 2,600 pounds (1,180 kg) of weight inside the aircraft and 8,000 pounds (3,630 kg) outside.

Glossary

aircraft carrier A military vehicle that carries aircraft and acts as a runway for them to take off or land

armed To have a weapon

armed forces A country's group of soldiers who fight on the ground, at sea, and in the air

armor A protective covering

combat A battle between enemies

crew A group of people who work together

enemy A force that works against a person or a country

hover To stay in one place in the air

information A collection of facts gathered from watching or studying

launcher A machine that shoots weapons such as missiles or rockets

rotate To turn in a circular direction

sensors Devices that detect and react to heat, cold, light, or motion

underwater mine A bomb that sits under the surface of the water and explodes when touched by ships or submarines

workhorse A term to describe someone or something that is suited to doing a number of jobs

Index